DAVID MOSES & MAX HELMER

A CEO'S GUIDE FOR
INCREASED ROI

7 Strategies for Better Online Growth in 2022

GROWTEAM

Contents

What Are the Three Biggest Threats to Your Online Growth Right Now?

The digital age has changed how most of us do business. Now more than ever, keeping up with new technological improvements and innovations is critical for success. After a few decades of doing business in the digital marketing realm, we've mastered the tricks of the trade and we created this guide to share them with you.

This book focuses on three main threats to your online revenue and ways you can approach them while planning for the year ahead.

1. Marketplace sites like Amazon drive down margins and enable increased competition from manufacturers and suppliers.

2. Larger sites and big box stores drive up paid search costs and benefit from recent algorithm changes on search engines, making it harder to win paid ad auctions and bring in quality leads.

3. Internal marketing staff, SEO, and pay-per-click agencies continue to adapt their strategies to keep up with the evolving online search trends.

In more simplified terms, you're facing rising client acquisition costs, working harder and harder each year just to stay up-to-date, and trying to make sure all your "expert" resources really do all they can to help you. Does this situation sound familiar?

So what can be done to fix this cycle? Over the past decade, we have tracked the performance of thousands of small to medium sized e-commerce businesses and interviewed the CEO's of the top performing 1% to find out what they do to set themselves apart. With their experience combined with ours, here are Grow Team's top seven strategies for increasing your marketing ROI.

STRATEGY 1:

Identify Your Weaknesses

We've worked with hundreds of CEOs over the years. From our experience, we've learned that everyone has their own opinion on the value of outsourcing services versus internal staffing. For important functions considered a core part of their business model, many business owners make an effort to hire full-time employees in-house. With these tasks completed by full-time employees, you can be sure of better oversight and management of the work done for your own business or customers. This approach also allows you to retain accumulated knowledge and intellectual properties should an employee be terminated or leave their position.

If you operate a business that depends on the internet for a large portion of its leads and revenue, it's easy to extend this same logic to online marketing initiatives. Depending on the size of your organization and the amount of revenue your online efforts generate, you may have a single person or a small team managing your website, social media channels, and email marketing campaigns. While large companies can often sustain a completely in-house marketing staff, for the majority of businesses this isn't always the smartest or most inexpensive solution.

So why would you consider outsourcing in order to compete digitally? We want to highlight 3 main reasons:

1. Rapid platform evolution — best practices, platforms, software, tools, etc. constantly change.

2. Accelerated training requirements — agencies must stay on top of changes in the industry and continuously train their employees to get good results.

3. The use of specialized software — tools used by agencies to gain an advantage that other businesses don't have.

Rapid Platform Evolution

While it may vary from industry to industry, there will always be a myriad of standard platforms you'll need to promote your business. Even the most common ones, like Google, and social media channels like LinkedIn and Facebook, require a deft hand to utilize effectively. Best practices for these platforms and others constantly change, with new updates and features to enhance your campaigns. For in-house employees, this requires more time spent learning how to stay up-to-date with changing regulations and requirements. Lack of awareness or a failure to engage on any critical platform can mean you're not reaching target customers. In order to be effective, outsourced agencies need to stay up-to-date on each of these changes so business owners don't need to, making outsourcing an attractive option.

Accelerated Training Requirements

Because platforms change at such a rapid pace, the training employees need in order to keep their skills current also evolves regularly. Training on a new platform can be incredibly expensive and requires a serious time investment. Most employees simply do not have the bandwidth to complete the training requirements while also doing the work assigned to them. Professional marketing firms often financially support this kind of training for their own employees, but many small businesses don't have the time or budget. Again, outsourcing covers these costs and time investments for you, which means when a contracted employee shows up to work, they already know how to effectively do their job.

The Use of Specialized Software

As the number of platforms and marketing channels companies use keeps growing, the need to monitor brand assets, coordinate content, and optimize ad buying across those channels also increases in importance. Many agencies have created or invested in specially-designed software to make these processes simpler, or pay hefty licensing fees to have a popular system do it for them. While these tools give organizations a leg-up over their less sophisticated competitors, lots of smaller businesses can't afford to use them, making outsourcing resources a more affordable choice.

What Should You Do?

These dynamics have driven a significant increase in outsourcing, especially when it comes to tech-based services. While it may seem appealing to have full-time employees managing some of these duties, it is necessary to complete a realistic assessment of their skills and available work hours. If your employees lack the necessary training or would become stretched too thin from too many tasks, looking to outside partners may be the best option for your business.

POWER QUESTIONS FOR EMPLOYEES

- What tasks take up the most energy and time each week? Could outsourcing some of the important or technical-driven tasks help you accomplish more revenue-driven work?

- What tasks do you feel qualified to handle? What tasks would benefit from outsourcing expertise?

POWER QUESTIONS FOR OUTSOURCING AGENCIES & CONTRACTORS

- What software or systems would you use to accomplish my most important tasks?

- How do you ensure you or your employees stay current when systems, programs, or algorithms change?

STRATEGY 2:

Focus on ROI, Not Cost

As a CEO, you work with a lot of different people. It can be easy to
get lost in the day to day when you constantly work through internal issues,
outside contractors, other business associates, and handling the day-to-day
operations. We've seen this mindset lead to many CEOs focusing solely
on the budget rather than the ROI of a project, and that's a problem.

Successful executives start by asking the right questions that lead to a blueprint
for success:

POWER QUESTIONS

- What will it take to increase our sales in this area by X% over the
  next 12 months?

- Given our business size and position in relation to our competitors,
  how much do we really need to invest to effectively compete? Which
  areas (SEO, paid search, social, mobile, affiliate, etc.) should we focus
  our investments?

- Given my product and service set, the current positioning and budget,
  what activities will generate the highest ROI ?

- How can we ensure that as we continue down our path that we
  quickly eliminate non-performing activities and focus our dollars on
  profitable ones? What metrics should we use to identify these high
  performing initiatives?

- What is a reasonable expectation of overall ROI for the investments I make?

Playing to Win

Generally, business owners don't get the results they want from their initiatives because they're not asking the right questions. They focus mainly on budget rather than getting an accurate picture of the needed investment that will generate a positive ROI over an amount of time. Because your company competes directly with others that also invest in the same kinds of services, this becomes even more difficult.

Many companies fail because they invest too little and try to take on major competitors with too little ammunition. Your trusted advisors will tell you when you're underestimating the task, but watch out for those who will take your money and give you false hope your plan will succeed while knowing it won't. Remember the age old adage of promises that seem too good to be true? Always beware of those who overpromise. And always ask for concrete proof and case studies before investing in these solutions.

If you use outside contractors to assist your business, you also need to calculate the additional costs on your end to support that work the agency does. You may need to spend additional staff time to augment their efforts and implement recommendations. It's important to factor these costs into your overall budget as well as your ROI calculations so you get a true sense of the return. Think about it like this, "What do I need to invest into a program so that I achieve my goals for ROI? What will it take to become relevant enough to attract clients and build significant ROI?"

For example, say you want to enter a marathon. You talk to a trainer and say, "I want you to train me for a marathon, but I'm only willing to spend two hours a week on it." A trainer who is desperate for money and doesn't really care will say, "Ok, sure. I'll work with you for whatever time you have. I'll put together a plan and we'll get started next week." But a master trainer who really knows what they're doing will look at you and tell you they won't waste their time on someone who isn't dedicated and likely won't even finish the race. There are many digital marketing agencies that will charge a lower fee for a service that will do little to no good. It's worth finding the right company with the right experience that will get you results.

A CASE STUDY: ROI VS. INITIAL SPENDING

A client who runs a professional services firm came to us after consistently making about $1,000,000 in online sales per year. Sales had been flat for a while and they were looking for ways to increase revenue. When we spoke to them originally, we talked with them about what they wanted to accomplish. They had worked with an agency for the past two years and the CEO was adamant that he wasn't willing to increase their budget or investment any further.

We got into a deep conversation with the CEO about his objectives and defined his goals for growth. It became clear he needed a different kind of partner. He needed a partner that could do more comprehensive work than the company he currently worked with. However, the work needed to reach his growth goals was going to be more expensive. In fact, doing what he wanted to do would almost double the budget he currently set.

The conversation turned to ROI versus budget. Over the course of our discussions, we realized he would see significant increases in sales by adopting a different strategy with a different partner, but it would require additional investment. Ultimately, he took our advice and decided to go with our recommended agency. The additional cost was $3,000/month more than what he previously paid. With the new program in place, his sales tripled!

We calculated the ROI, which earned this company almost a 900% return. A truly significant win for this CEO who realized that he couldn't have this kind of growth with a fixed budget.

STRATEGY 3:

Set Clear Expectations

After hiring and managing thousands of employees and negotiating hundreds of marketing service contracts, we've found two reasons normally responsible for poor contract relationships. Those are a lack of specific deliverables, and lack of specific communication expectations.

Lack of Specific Deliverables

When outsourcing to an agency or independent contractor, you normally expect to receive a defined deliverable. It can look like a set amount of created content, a number of managed products, a certain increase in ROI, etc. However, while these deliverables may be agreed upon verbally, they must also be defined in a written contract. This is your responsibility as the project manager or company owner. It is imperative that the signed contract you share with your outsourced employees expressly stipulates what you and your business will receive.

POWER QUESTIONS

- How can I quantify the work you're doing? What specific work can I expect completed on my behalf every month?

- After the first phase of implementation, what kind of timetable will we use? What deliverables will I receive on an ongoing basis?

Lack of Specific Communication Expectations

Planned deliverables will solve some of your problems, but without a communication schedule, even the best-laid plans can quickly fall apart. Determine how often you'll speak with your contracted workers. While "as-needed" communication can often be a go-to for some agencies, push for a stricter communication timeline. With predictable check-in times, be they weekly, bi-weekly, or monthly, you and your contracted workers know what to expect and will remain accountable for outstanding action items.

POWER QUESTIONS

- Who will be my point of contact during our partnership? How often will we communicate?

- What should my team prepare before a scheduled call or meeting to make them as productive as possible? What information do you need from me in order to be successful?

STRATEGY 4:

Get a Good Account Manager

While working with any outside agency, you will have different people you'll be in contact with throughout the process. You'll speak with a salesperson up front and could possibly have different customer service representatives you touch base with along the way. Or if it's a smaller agency, perhaps you're speaking with the owner who made the sale and then handles the work. Either way, be clear on who you will be communicating with throughout the contract.

Avoid Falling for the Salesperson

If you have contracted out different marketing services in the past, then you know some of the worst companies sometimes have the best sales people. They know exactly what to say, and have expert experience selling the big brands and experience of their firm. In the sales process, they talk about the work they've done for brands like Honda, Nike, IBM, or any other big brand, then supplement that experience with white papers and other collateral. If you really focus on this aspect of their pitch, you'll probably think, "Wow, these guys must really know their stuff. Honda wouldn't work with just anyone." If they truly are working with these big brands, then the best account managers go to these big brands, ones probably much bigger than yours. These sales people build rapport and confidence with you and convince you that everyone on their team will be just as good when you might get different service levels for a smaller package.

We're not here to knock legitimate salespeople and the work they do. But a lot of companies in the online marketing space have adopted a business model that specifically focuses their resources on sales at the direct expense of service, because they believe it is cheaper to acquire new clients than it is to retain them. This is the "churn-and-burn" model at its greatest (or worst). We strongly recommend vetting your actual account manager who handles the day to day work long before you sign a contract. Because when it's all said and done, your account manager will be the one you depend on to get results for your business.

The Importance of Account Manager Selection

As part of the build-out of our national network, we have evaluated thousands of companies and hundreds of individual account managers within those companies. We have gone into online marketing companies and invested the time to better understand account management structure and its impact on performance.

We learned that 99% of the success of your relationship with an online marketing company is determined by your specific account manager. We found that when a sales manager closes a new account, it goes into a lottery system for account manager assignment based on which one has the most availability. Newer, less experienced account managers who don't yet have a full book of business get a majority of newly signed clients. We see this especially for small businesses who sign with a large agency.

Account Managers Drive Your Experience and Results

It may seem obvious, but not all account managers are created equal. Our experience and research has shown us that most companies have very little formal or ongoing training. Nor do many have fixed procedures related to the communication cycles and work which account managers put into individual accounts. This results in an extremely high correlation between campaign performance and individual account manager assignments.

After evaluating the performance of hundreds of campaigns, we found account managers who consistently ranked at the top end of the scale not only increased the performance of the campaigns they supervise, but also retained their clients longer. They had more frequent communication, better follow-up, and generally more happy clients because of the high level of service.

So How Do I Get a Good Account Manager?

It's very simple. Just ask for one! More specifically, tell the agency that you need to know who your account manager will be before you sign the contract. Talk to your new account manager, interview them, even look up their background. What are their values? What's their skill set and expertise? Ask specific questions about your business, website, or campaign and how they plan to help improve it. If you don't like the answers, ask for a different representative from the start.

POWER QUESTIONS

- What experience do you have with the specific services I'm contracting for?

- What training and certifications do you have?

- Have you worked on similar-sized accounts in the past?

- What is your plan to increase revenue for my business? Why?

- What's the best way for us to communicate regularly?

What if You Think You Have a Bad Account Manager?

Demand to switch. If you're not happy you should do this immediately. Wasting time trying to make a bad account manager into a good one isn't your problem.

It's a training issue that the agency needs to address. You need never be shy about calling the senior manager at an agency and asking for a new account manager if you're not happy with the results you're getting or there is a lack of good communication.

Remember, it's absolutely acceptable to evaluate the company you're going to contract with. More than just acceptable, it's necessary. You need to evaluate it all the way down to the actual account manager you'll be working with. Or you risk wasting your time and money on the performance of the entire campaign. Don't be dazzled by their client list, collateral, and Powerpoint decks. Focus on the people that will actually do the work for you.

STRATEGY 5:

Learn How to Quickly Identify the Bad Apples

Like a lot of business dealings, working with outside agencies usually requires a bit of gut instinct. But knowing what to look for can make weeding out the bad apples even easier. We've found three common "red flags" that may indicate an unhealthy partner relationship:

Lack of Transparency

In the simplest of terms, transparency is the ability to show and tell. A company that lacks transparency may refuse to show you various aspects of your campaign. Maybe they won't provide a reference sheet or can't show the work of what they've actually done for your website. If a company refuses to let you see the work they do on your behalf, the work (if you ever do see it) will most likely be subpar. For many underperforming agencies, keeping you in the dark is their best asset to keep you as a client.

Access to Accounts

Outsourcing account management may look desirable, but if a contracted firm or employee refuses to allow you access to those accounts, you may be in danger. Companies who engage in this practice will often say they manage a particular account under their own master account or through an internal system. Don't believe them. If you pay for a third party service, you should have access to your account at all times. This isn't just to manage the revenue these projects may be creating. In order to make informed business decisions over time, you need accurate information about your accounts.

Falsified Reporting

In order to track the success of any marketing campaign, a reporting system must be in place. If your contractors refuse to show you any reporting data, this is a warning sign. SEO is usually the most likely place for false reporting, with agencies generating reports that are either overly complicated or outright fabrications. Every reporting document, regardless of its subject, should be easy enough for you to understand or for the account manager to explain. If you cannot understand the reports, or your account manager cannot break down the details in a way you can understand, there's probably a reason.

A CASE STUDY: WHY ASKING THE RIGHT QUESTIONS MATTERS

A while ago, a business owner came to us with some confusion about his current marketing agency. He said, "My marketing company is doing a good job, but I'm still not seeing the increase in sales I thought I would." When we asked how he had come to that conclusion, the client showed us a report created by the agency he had hired.

The report showed the client had 65 "conversions" on his paid search campaign from the last month, which the agency had classified as completed sales from clients who had clicked through on paid ads. However, the client reported that the site had only processed 43 sales in total in the same period. "I just don't know why things aren't adding up," he told us. "I mean, the numbers from Google can't be wrong, can they?"

We called the agency to do some digging, and began by asking direct questions about the "conversions" tracking they completed. We also asked them about the AdWords account they had started on behalf of our client. It quickly became apparent the agency made several mistakes with the tracking pixels on this particular campaign, and that the real conversion numbers on the client's pay-per-click campaign (PPC) were much lower. Whether it was true or not, they could not explain how the mistakes had occurred or why they had been reporting numbers that weren't correlated to the Google Analytics reports for several months.

Due to these errors, the relationship between the two firms was short-lived, and we quickly found our new client a business partner from our network to accomplish the tasks initially given to the original agency.

Getting on the Right Side

Your long-term business strategy should be based on industry-standard best practices and align with the specific interests and abilities of the platforms you use. If you ask the right high-level questions, you will arrive at the right conclusions, and you will find it easier to spot a bad apple from a good one.

Ethical companies will train their employees and contractors to be ethical too. Companies and employees who are dedicated to "white-hat" tactics will employ things like alignment, best practices, and industry guidelines when making decisions and crafting a strategy. They will not use words like "gaming", "tricking", or "masking", and they won't suggest you dedicate time creating junk content or engaging with partnerships whose policies and procedures are not above board. They do not make promises they are unable to keep, and they do not make guarantees about things they cannot control. Avoid the temptation to go for the quickest, easiest solution—if something sounds too good to be true, it usually is.

POWER QUESTIONS

- Do the strategies your firm uses benefit the end user?

- Do the action items completed by the agency create a better user experience on both a search engine and our website?

STRATEGY 6:

Be Careful When Seeking Advice

Good Intentions, Bad Advice

As your business strategy evolves over time, you have to be conscious of who you ask for advice. If you work with an outside firm that specializes mainly in social media marketing, they're likely to emphasize social media and push you into spending more money and strategizing in that area. The same situation would play out with a pay-per-click company, an SEO company, an affiliate marketing company, etc. Given this fact, it's critical that you seek out input and advice from people who don't have a vested interest in one specific type of service or marketing platform and can help you decide what will be best for your company.

It can be extremely helpful for business owners to get expert opinions about the overall strategy they wish to implement. Just asking agencies how they would approach things won't be enough since obviously they will be biased towards the types of services they provide. The advice these agencies offer isn't meant to be spiteful or given in malice, it's honestly just because that's what they know. They believe in their industry and the solutions they provide.

Aside from specific vendor bias, it's also important to be aware of a constantly changing marketplace. In previous chapters in this book, we talked about ROI being the metric that's most important. As you track ROI, you will see certain types of activities drive higher ROI than others as time goes along. When you see these trends emerge, it's often in your best interest to move investment dollars from one type of activity to another. Unfortunately, if it means losing a contract, most agencies won't be eager to notify you of these trends.

Search for the Highest ROI Use of Funds

As a business leader, your question shouldn't be "Can I make a positive ROI on this activity?" Instead, ask this power question: "Is this activity the highest ROI activity available to me right now?"

Asking the latter question forces you to analyze multiple options and evaluate the potential returns that you could receive. If you ask an agency or someone specifically involved in one aspect of online marketing, they're very likely to tell you about what they do most often – the solution that worked for them. To that person, their solution will also work for you. However, with so many differences between each industry and their unique businesses, there is no one size fits all. We also recommend you ask this question broadly for your business and even while considering traditional marketing opportunities like print advertising and direct sales.

A CASE STUDY: INVESTING IN THE BEST ROI ACTIVITY FOR YOU

One of our current clients, an e-commerce specialty products company, came to us spending five figures a month on pay-per-click ads and $3,500 a month on an SEO company that did content marketing for them. We looked at the overall investment they made each month, how the campaigns performed, and the blended cost of traffic. We ended up recommending they reallocate their content marketing budget into a contract with a new partner for a specific type of technical SEO work. We also recommended they overhaul and restructure their paid search program.

By making those changes, that company was able to increase organic traffic by 35% in just 90 days. That created an additional $30,000 per month in sales. So by lowering their blended cost of acquisition overall, they were able to be even more competitive with their paid search campaigns. They then expanded their reach into new ad networks and were able to drastically increase ROI. Getting quality outside advice and perspective on your marketing programs proves to be well worth the effort.

STRATEGY 7:

Learn to Manage Integration

As the owner or manager of a business, you have a responsibility to create an integration system between internal resources and outside agencies. Your success in this endeavor will impact how you leverage the dollars you invest in a digital marketing service. We've identified four best practices to consider when designing an integration system: establishing communication loops, leveraging your resources, creating a team mentality, and sharing vital information.

Establish Communication Loops

You need to establish two specific communication loops with an online marketing partner:

1. A regular, scheduled call to review reports and discuss upcoming action items, this call should include your internal marketing staff, and they should come prepared with questions to sync everyone's priorities.

2. Direct, impromptu communication via email and phone between your staff and your account manager. This is especially important when you launch new products or services, implement changes to your website, or hold seasonal specials or events.

The account manager for your organization will most likely have experience working with other clients and experience in your industry that can help them implement best practices with ease. These contracted employees have varying levels of experience, so simply asking good questions can give you great information.

POWER QUESTIONS FOR YOUR AGENCY

- What are some of the best practices for this type of work?

- What practices, ideas, or solutions are working for your other clients? Can you implement some of these for us?

- What trends have you seen emerge in the past few months or years that may be relevant to our business?

- What do you think we can do to increase our conversions?

- If you were in our position, what would you do that we are not?

Leverage Your Resources With Your Agency's Expertise

Although outsourcing work generally means less responsibility for you, it would be foolish to leave your marketing partner without any resources you have at your disposal. With any extra data or tools, you could give your contracted agency an improved ability to deliver the results you're looking for. In addition to supplying your contracted agency with any extra resources, we recommend you learn the best practices and industry knowledge to better understand the success of your campaigns and retain a solid understanding if you ever stop working with them.

POWER QUESTIONS FOR YOUR AGENCY

- What can my team do to accelerate your work?

- Where would you recommend we devote our resources if you had access to my team's time?

- How can our team be more involved with our online marketing campaign so our efforts have a higher chance of success?

- What can we do on a weekly and monthly basis to enhance your efforts?

Create a Team Mentality

After finalizing an agreement with a new partner, incorporate them as a full-fledged member of your team as best as you can. Just like you would with internal employees, integrate your agency's account manager into communication cycles that include your internal planning meeting, and encourage them to become invested in your long-term success. Remember that your success is also their success. A mutually beneficial long-term agreement is the goal. The more they like you and appreciate your business, the harder they'll work to keep you.

Share Vital Information

Agencies need accurate data to succeed, and if you're able to provide it to them, you should do so. Sharing information breeds trust and common accountability to the goals you share. It also helps protect against an agency hiding mistakes or shielding data.

PRACTICAL IDEAS FOR YOU & YOUR STAFF

- Learn how to read and understand analytic data yourself. Ask detailed questions about your traffic and conversions to help you comprehend it clearly.

- Provide Google certifications to some of your internal team members. This will give your team the ability to understand what agencies do and how they can help them succeed. The certification is not expensive, and can give your team a competitive edge.

- Set up bi-weekly or monthly calls or meetings. Ask your team to come to these events with a summary of their completed action items and questions about how to proceed going forward.

Stay Connected at the Top

This is our final recommendation: talk to the CEO of each of your agencies at least once a year. Tell them about your experience with their team and how they're impacting your future revenue goals. Ask them about their thoughts and experiences within your shared industry, and what general trends they see that could affect you. Simply scheduling a call with the CEO will trigger an internal review of your campaigns, a status update from their team, and ensure everyone who has a hand in your company's account with their firm is communicating with the right people. It also gives you much-needed visibility at the top level, and puts you front-of-mind with senior executives, who may have insider introductions or recommendations that could benefit you and your business.

Why We Wrote This Book

As entrepreneurs ourselves, we have a very personal connection to the challenges of a growing business. We've spent years learning marketing, hiring and firing agencies, making money, losing money, and struggling to keep up with the rapidly changing landscape of online marketing and e-commerce. We have also struggled to learn when to hire internal staff or outsource to an agency, as well as how to effectively manage them and their work.

Driven by our frustrations and learning experiences from these challenges, we created Grow Team, the first national quality and performance vetting service for online marketing companies. Starting from a simple idea to find the best specialist agencies in the country, we work to help companies get great deals from these agencies and ensure they get the results they expect. Since its inception, Grow Team has evaluated and thoroughly vetted hundreds of online marketing companies. We have matched thousands of small and medium-sized businesses with trusted marketing companies to help set them up for success. We are the first true buyer's agency for online marketing services and continue to grow our national presence at a rapid pace.

This book is our way of sharing the knowledge and experience we've gained as fellow business owners and from negotiating hundreds of online marketing service contracts for small-medium sized businesses.

People often ask us if giving away our knowledge actually undermines our businesses. And the answer is definitely a no. By telling people about what we do, and by sharing our experiences, we can help business owners better manage the process for themselves. We hope we were able to inspire you to look for new opportunities for your business's growth and answer any questions you might have been searching for. We are dedicated not just to your business's success, but to helping you achieve the best possible results. If you have any questions about how anything from this book can apply to your business, we invite you to give us a call or visit our website and take advantage of our years of knowledge and experience. If you haven't done much marketing, aren't happy with the results you might be getting from your current agency, or are just looking for new growth opportunities, we hope to hear from you soon. From all of us here at Grow Team, we wish you and your business the best!

About the Authors

David Moses

David Moses is an experienced executive with a history of leadership roles in both early stage entrepreneurial organizations and established private equity-backed groups.

He has extensive experience building sales programs, increasing online revenue, building brands, and improving operations through a disciplined, metrics-driven approach.

David is passionate about helping other business owners succeed in a rapidly changing environment and he's dedicated to the long term success of our clients.

Originally from New York, David has two amazing daughters and currently resides in San Diego. David has served on several industry boards and was chairman and a board member of the charity Gift for Life.

Max Helmer

Max Helmer is a senior executive with experience in all aspects of early stage company growth. He has an in-depth understanding of the online and digital marketing industry as well as SaaS applications.

He has a broad base of experience in negotiating and managing contracts with outside suppliers, focused on generating long term performance and results.

Max was born and raised in San Diego and loves working with small business owners to help them grow their companies.

QUESTIONS?

We help companies find the best partners at the

best price. If you'd like us to evaluate your business

and make strategic recommendations, just give us

a call and tell us that you read our book.

GROW TEAM MAIN OFFICE
800-741-9298

OR VISIT
GROWTEAM.COM

60247997R00020